NATIONAL
GEOGRAPHIC
KiDS

Just Joking 5

5

300
hilarious
jokes about
everything,
including
tongue
twisters,
riddles, and
more!

by Rosie Gowsell-Pattison

NATIONAL GEOGRAPHIC
WASHINGTON, D.C.

The Galápagos tortoise can live to be over 100 years old and weigh more than 800 pounds (362 kg)!

KNOCK, KNOCK.

Who's there?
Spine.
Spine who?
Quit spine on me!

Snow leopards have wide paws to help them walk on top of the snow.

6

Say this fast three times:

Seventy-seven silly superstitions.

Q Why didn't the teddy bear finish his dinner?

A Because he was stuffed.

7

TONGUE TWISTER!

Say this fast three times:

Wicked winter winds wreak wreckage.

Q What do you call a sweet snack that won the lottery?

A A fortune cookie.

Q Why are sodas always so successful?

A Because they have a can-do attitude.

Q What is a **magician's** favorite **cereal?**

A Trix.

Hoary marmots are sometimes called "whistle pigs" because of the high-pitched whistle they use to alert their colony to trouble.

KNOCK, KNOCK.

Who's there?
Mayan.
Mayan who?
Never mayan, I'll come back later.

9

10

Collies were traditionally bred
to herd cattle and sheep.

Q What do camels wear when they play hide-and-seek?

A Camel-flage.

Q What did one tornado say to the other tornado?

A See you around!

Take a deep breath! Seals can stay underwater for up to 30 minutes before they need to come up for air.

KNOCK, KNOCK.

Who's there?
Anakin.
Anakin who?
Anakin you can do, I can do better.

13

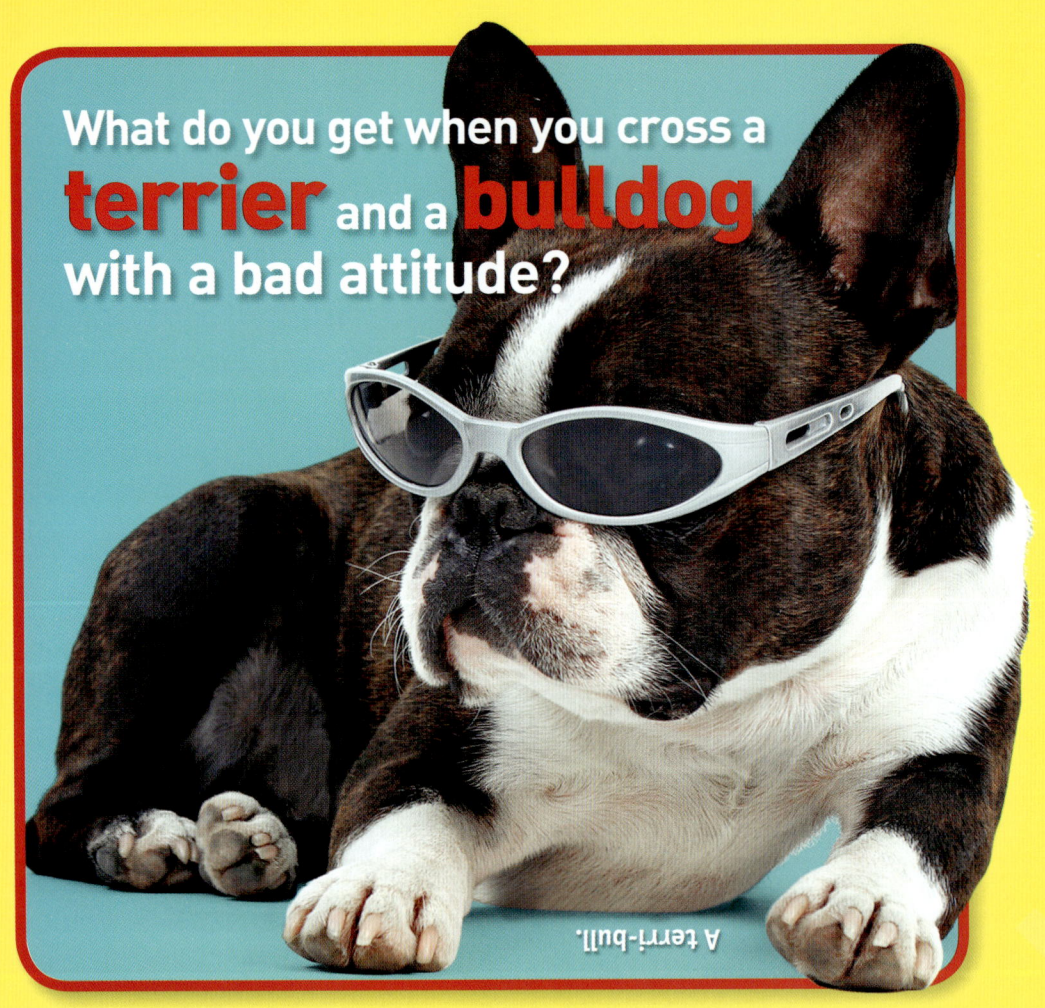

What do you get when you cross a **terrier** and a **bulldog** with a bad attitude?

A terri-bull.

Say this fast three times:

Selfish shellfish.

Q

What kind of **dinosaur** loves **English class?**

A thesaurus.

A

Q What do you say to a rodent when it leaves for work?

A Have a mice day!

Q Why are petri dishes so smart?

A Because they're very cultured.

TONGUE TWISTER!

Say this fast three times:

The big beautiful blue balloon burst.

Baboons have a loud bark that sounds like "Wahoo!"

KNOCK, KNOCK.

Who's there?
Meow.
Meow who?
Open this door right meow!

18

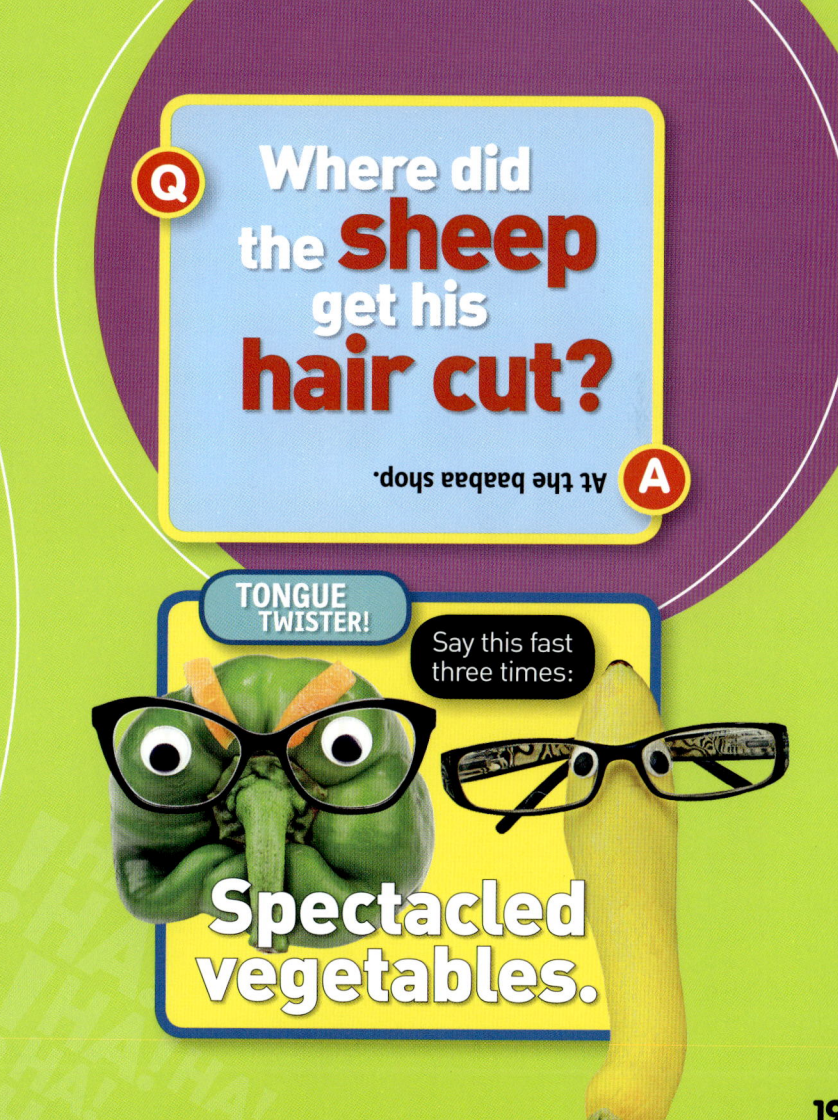

Q Where did the **sheep** get his get his **hair cut?**

A At the baabaa shop.

TONGUE TWISTER!

Say this fast three times:

Spectacled vegetables.

Q What do you call a dog that talks on the phone all day?

A A call-ie.

Q What kind of **animal** loves to eat **bread?**

A A carbivore.

Q How do trees feel in the springtime?

A Re-leaved.

Q What do you call a cat that gets caught stealing?

A The purr-petrator.

No sweater? No problem! Polar bears have nearly 4 inches (10 cm) of blubber under their skin to keep them warm.

21

Cotton-top tamarins are one of the most endangered primates in the world.

23

This looker is a Taiwan beauty snake. They are named for their colorful and beautifully patterned bodies.

KNOCK, KNOCK.

Who's there?
Metaphors.
Metaphors who?
Metaphors be with you.

Q Why did the kitten want to be left alone?

A Because he was in a bad mew-ed.

Q What advice did the **blood bank manager** have for her staff?

A B positive. This job can be draining.

Q What is a ghost's favorite lunch?

A A boo-loney sandwich.

Q What did one toilet say to the other?

A You look a bit flushed.

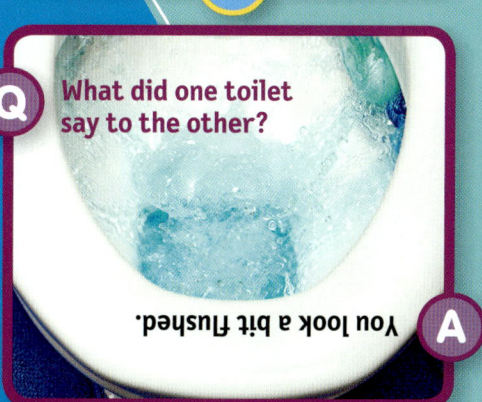

25

Q What do you call a grumpy ex–hockey player?

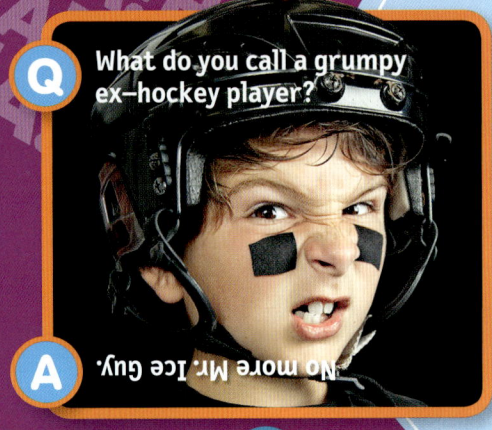

A No more Mr. Ice Guy.

Q What kind of **cereal** do **cats** like to **eat**?

A Mice Krispies.

Q What kind of **video game system** do **witches** use?

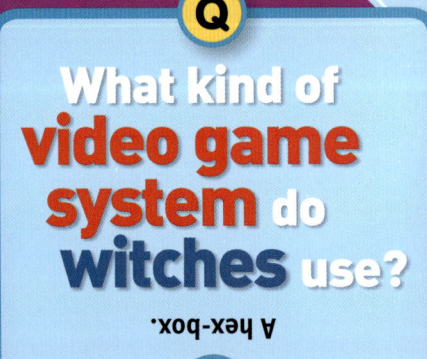

A A hex-box.

Q What kind of insect listens to music?

A A rockroach.

Bulldogs can't swim. With their large heads, heavy bodies, and short legs, they can't even dog paddle.

27

What did the cupcake do on vacation?

Muffin much.

A mouse opossum's tail is as long as its body!

KNOCK, KNOCK.

Who's there?
Squidding.
Squidding who?
You've got to be squidding me right now!

Q Why won't the **cannibal** eat **feet?**

A Because he's lack-toes intolerant.

Q What do **pirate beauty queens** wear?

A Ti-arrr-as.

31

Q What do you call a singing cow?

A Britney Steers.

Q What do you call a crazy chicken?

A Hen-sane.

Q Why can't the **rapper** put his **rhinestone jacket** in the **dryer?**

A Because it will get static bling.

Q Which **Renaissance painter** had a **sweet tooth?**

A Donut-ello.

Zebras can run at speeds of up to 35 miles per hour (56 kph).

KNOCK,

KNOCK.

Who's there?
Heifer.
Heifer who?
Are you heifer
going to be ready
to leave?

34

The American mink gives off an unpleasant odor if it is threatened or scared.

35

Which dog swims and solves mysteries?

Scuba Dooby Doo.

PORCUPINE 1:
Do you like my new hat?

PORCUPINE 2:
Lookin' sharp!

Q What kind of bird is bad at catching fish?

A A pelican't.

Q What do you call a sleeping dancer?

A A slumber-ina.

TONGUE TWISTER!

Say this fast three times:

I seldom smell a scent similar to the scent I suddenly smelled.

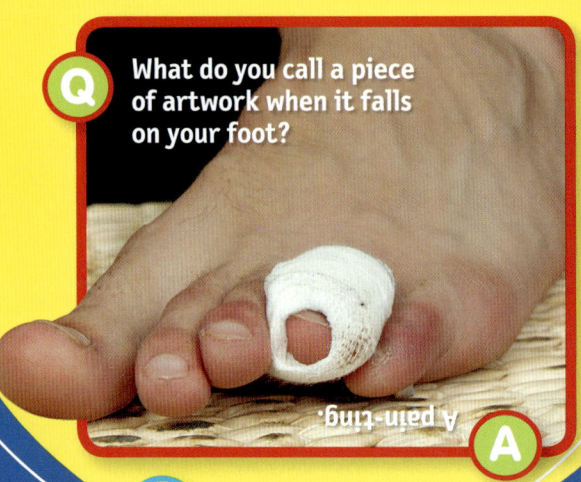

Q What do you call a piece of artwork when it falls on your foot?

A A pain-ting.

Q What do you call a **sold-out** **Mother's Day** **brunch?**

 A Maxi-mom capacity.

Hey, keep it down! A lion's roar can be heard up to 5 miles (8 km) away.

KNOCK, KNOCK.

Who's there?
Cannoli.
Cannoli who?
I cannoli imagine you aren't ready to go yet?

Say this fast three times:

Four fine fillies flitted their forelocks.

Bald eagles have excellent eyesight. They can spot a fish while flying up to a mile (1.6 km) overhead!

Why do **eagles** make great talent show **contestants?**

Because they are very talon-ted.

Q What treats do zombies like to bake?

A Brain muffins.

Q What sports competition do polar bears compete in?

A The Snowlympics.

DJ 1: Oh no! My favorite headphones are broken!

DJ 2: Can't you just get new ones?

DJ 1: No, those were ear-replaceable.

43

KNOCK, KNOCK.

Who's there?
Yam.
Yam who?
I yam so happy
to see you!

An elephant's trunk is strong enough to lift up to 450 pounds (204 kg) and agile enough to pluck a blade of grass.

Q What looks like half an orange?

A The other half.

Q

What kind of **Transformer** makes good **ice cream?**

A The Decepti-cones.

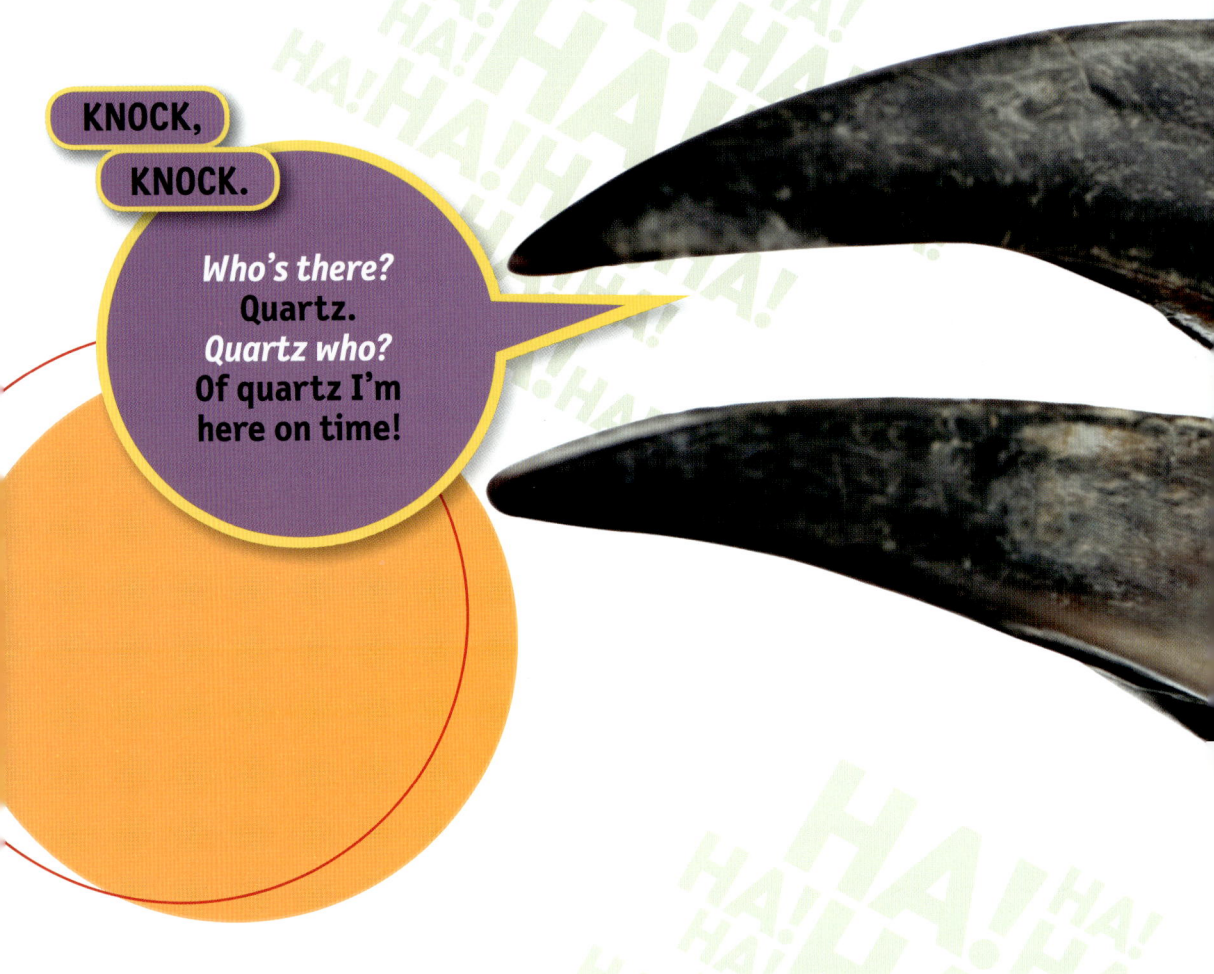

KNOCK, KNOCK.

Who's there?
Quartz.
Quartz who?
Of quartz I'm here on time!

Are you ever moving out? The southern ground hornbill can depend on its parents for up to two years, longer than any other bird.

Q Why did the cat take a test?

A He thought he would get a purr-fect score.

Q Why don't grizzlies make good comedians?

A Because their jokes are unbearable.

Q What do you call Hannah Montana with a head cold?

A Miley Virus.

WEDDING GUEST 1:
Why are you bringing that loaf of bread to the wedding?

WEDDING GUEST 2:
I want to toast the bride and groom.

48

How does a **snail** feel when it **loses** its **shell?**

A little sluggish.

missing

$$$
reward

An iguana's skin color will change depending on its mood.

KNOCK, KNOCK.

Who's there?
Cashew.
Cashew who?
Give me all the cashew have.

50

Q What does a dinosaur wear to a formal dinner?

A A tricera-top hat.

Q Which **zoo animal** is always **complaining?**

A The whine-ocerous.

Q What do reindeer ghosts say?

A Cari-boo!

Q Who is a pig's favorite superhero?

A Iron Ham.

51

The king vulture eats carrion, or dead and decaying flesh. They have powerful senses of smell and sight that allow them to find food from high up in the sky.

What does a vulture pack for a vacation?

Carrion luggage.

Wolves are the largest member of the dog family. The gray wolf can eat up to 20 pounds (9 kg) of meat in one meal!

Q What did the snake give birth to?

A A bouncing baby boa.

Q

How do you make anti-freeze?

A Steal her blanket.

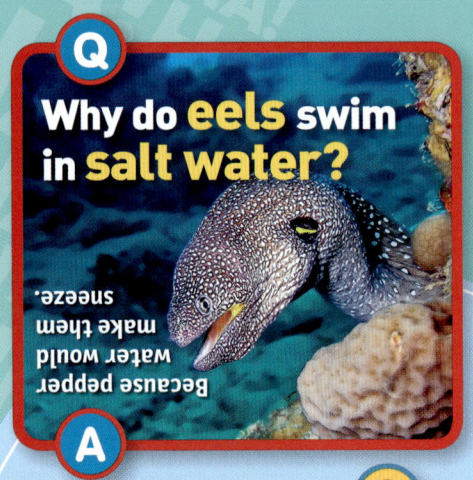

Q

Why do eels swim in salt water?

A Because pepper water would make them sneeze.

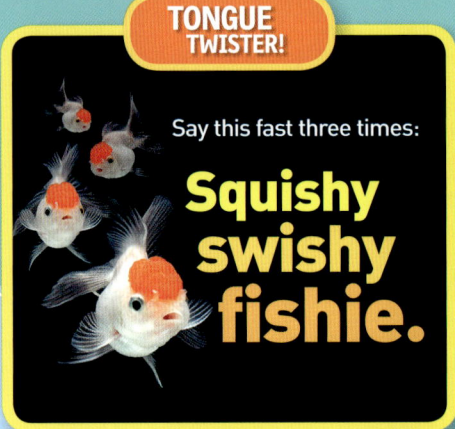

TONGUE TWISTER!

Say this fast three times:

Squishy swishy fishie.

Q

Where do sheep watch funny videos?

A On Ewe-Tube.

Q

Why will you always enjoy a hot drink from a marsupial?

A Because they only serve koala-tea.

Did you hear the joke about the pachyderm?

Never mind, it's irrelephant.

The lesser hedgehog tenrec may look like a hedgehog, but it is actually not part of the hedgehog family.

KNOCK,
KNOCK.

Who's there?
Turnip.
Turnip who?
Turnip the volume, this is my favorite song!

KNOCK, KNOCK.

Who's there?
Ben.
Ben who?
Ben ringing your doorbell for ten minutes!

The big-eyed tree frog turns from green to brown as it grows older.

Jude: What did you do when you found out your scooter was stolen?

Wyatt: I moped around.

Q

What do you call a sad superhero?

A

The Incredible Sulk.

Say this fast three times:

Larry loves Louise's luscious lasagna.

Q Why didn't the chickens cancel their picnic when it started to rain?

A Because they don't mind a little fowl weather.

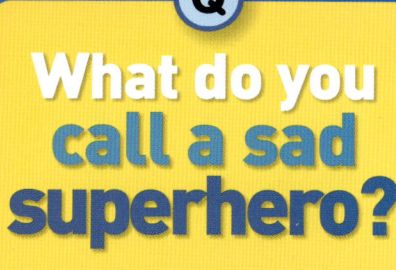

Q What is a **werewolf's** favorite **day** of the **week?**

A Moonday.

TONGUE TWISTER!

Say this fast three times:

A pest exists amidst us.

KNOCK, KNOCK.

Who's there?
Boris.
Boris who?
Are you going to boris with more knock-knock jokes?

Toucans have large bills for eating fruit but short wings, since they only fly short distances from tree to tree.

A walrus uses its tusks to help drag itself out of the water and for poking breathing holes in ice.

Why are walruses the life of the party?

Because they tell the sealiest jokes.

What a joker! The clown snake eel likes to bury itself in the sand and pop its head out in search of food.

KNOCK, KNOCK.

Who's there?
Army Ants.
Army Ants who?
Army ants and uncles coming for dinner?

Say this fast three times:

My newfangled bangles get jangled and tangled.

Q What did the insects name their band?

A The Black-Eyed Fleas.

67

Q

Why do **zombies** invite lots of friends to their **parties?**

A

Because the morgue the merrier!

CARRIE: I can't find my rutabaga!

CHARLOTTE: Don't worry, it will turnip.

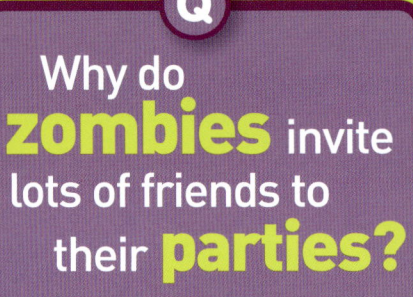

Q

What do you call a rabbit with fleas?

A

Bugs bunny.

Q

Why was the zoo happy to send their wildebeests away?

A

Because no gnus is good gnus.

Say this fast three times:

Shirley hurled a burly squirrel.

KNOCK, KNOCK.

Who's there?
Poppa.
Poppa who?
Poppa tire, do you have a spare?

Black-capped chickadees can usually be seen foraging for food upside down on branches and at bird feeders!

NICO: I am taking some of your cheese.

MACEO: Hey, leave my provolone!

What do you call a **police officer** in a garden?

Lawn and order.

A

Q Why do bakers work such long hours?

Because they are gluttens for punishment.

A

Arctic foxes have incredible hearing. They can hear prey tunneling underneath the snow.

73

Q Why can't you call the zoo on the phone?

A Because the lion is always busy.

Q

Where do sick fish go?

To the sturgeon.

A

TONGUE TWISTER!

Say this fast three times:

Wayne went to Wales to watch walruses.

Q Why do skunks make terrible waiters?

A Because their service stinks.

74

Where do bees go on vacation?

Pollenesia.

Say this fast three times:

Eight argyle gargoyles.

The ring-tailed coati makes woofing and clicking noises to alert others to predators.

KNOCK,

KNOCK.

Who's there?
Bison.
Bison who?
Wanna bison Girl
Scout cookies?

Q Why do ducks make great comedians?

A Because they can really quack you up.

TONGUE TWISTER!

Say this fast three times:

I ate at eight but snacked at seven and eleven.

HA! HA! HA! HA! HA! HA!

Where do most city horses live? Q

A In the neigh-borhood.

Say this fast three times:

Stu glued blue shoes.

FUNNY PUNS

Can a soup store ever be out of stock?

Q How did the cook feel when he found out his toaster wasn't waterproof?

A Shocked.

When baby horses, or foals, are born, their legs are too long for them to bend down to eat grass!

KNOCK, KNOCK.

Who's there?
Odor.
Odor who?
I'd like to odor a large pepperoni pizza.

Parrots are one of the most intelligent bird species. They are known for imitating the human voice.

83

A dog's sense of smell can be 1,000 times better than a human's.

KNOCK, KNOCK.

Who's there?
Heaven.
Heaven who?
Heaven seen you in ages!

84

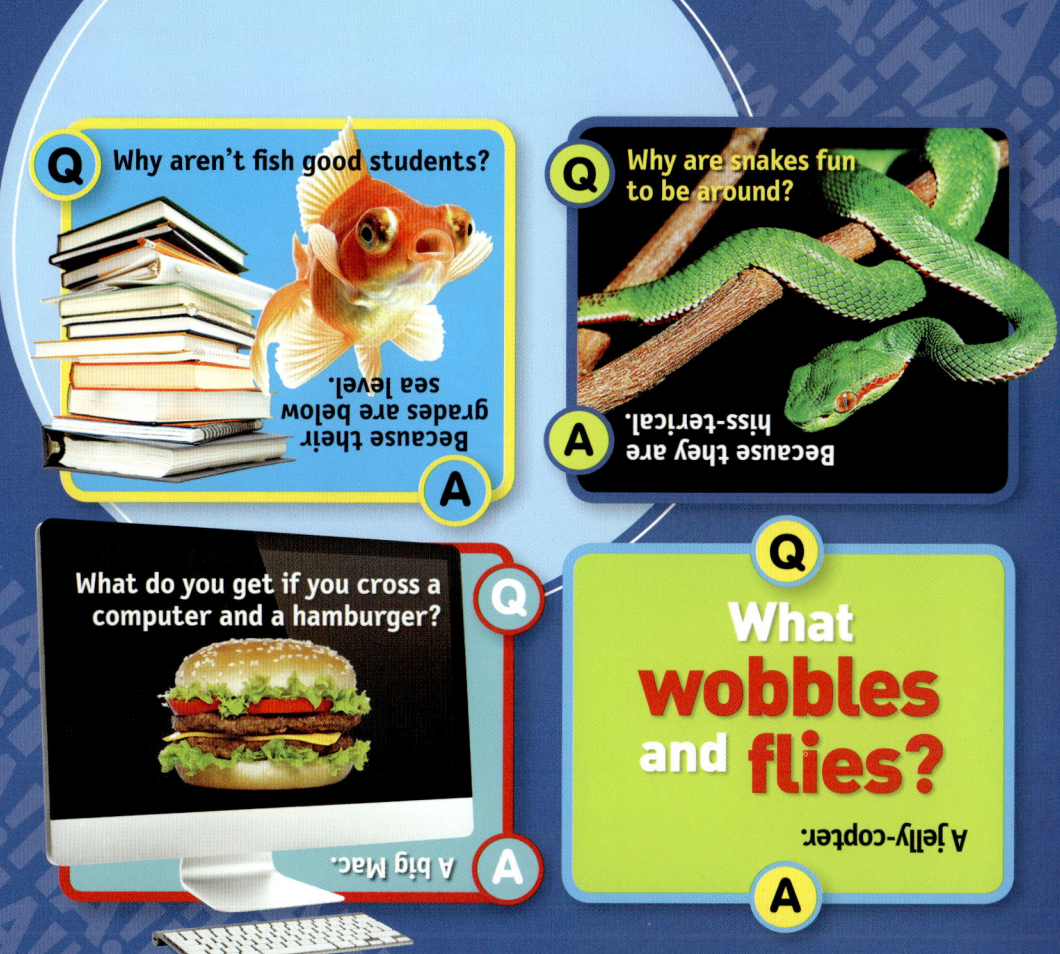

Q Why aren't fish good students?

A Because their grades are below sea level.

Q Why are snakes fun to be around?

A Because they are hiss-terical.

Q What do you get if you cross a computer and a hamburger?

A A big Mac.

Q What **wobbles** and **flies?**

A A jelly-copter.

Q

Why did the guitar player fall asleep on stage?

A He rocked himself to sleep

TONGUE TWISTER!

Say this fast three times:

Vera varnished while Pam polished.

KNOCK, KNOCK.

Who's there?
Raisin.
Raisin who?
Is there a raisin you aren't opening this door?

The great blue heron is the largest North American heron. It has a wingspan of 36 to 54 inches (91 to 137 cm).

TONGUE TWISTER!

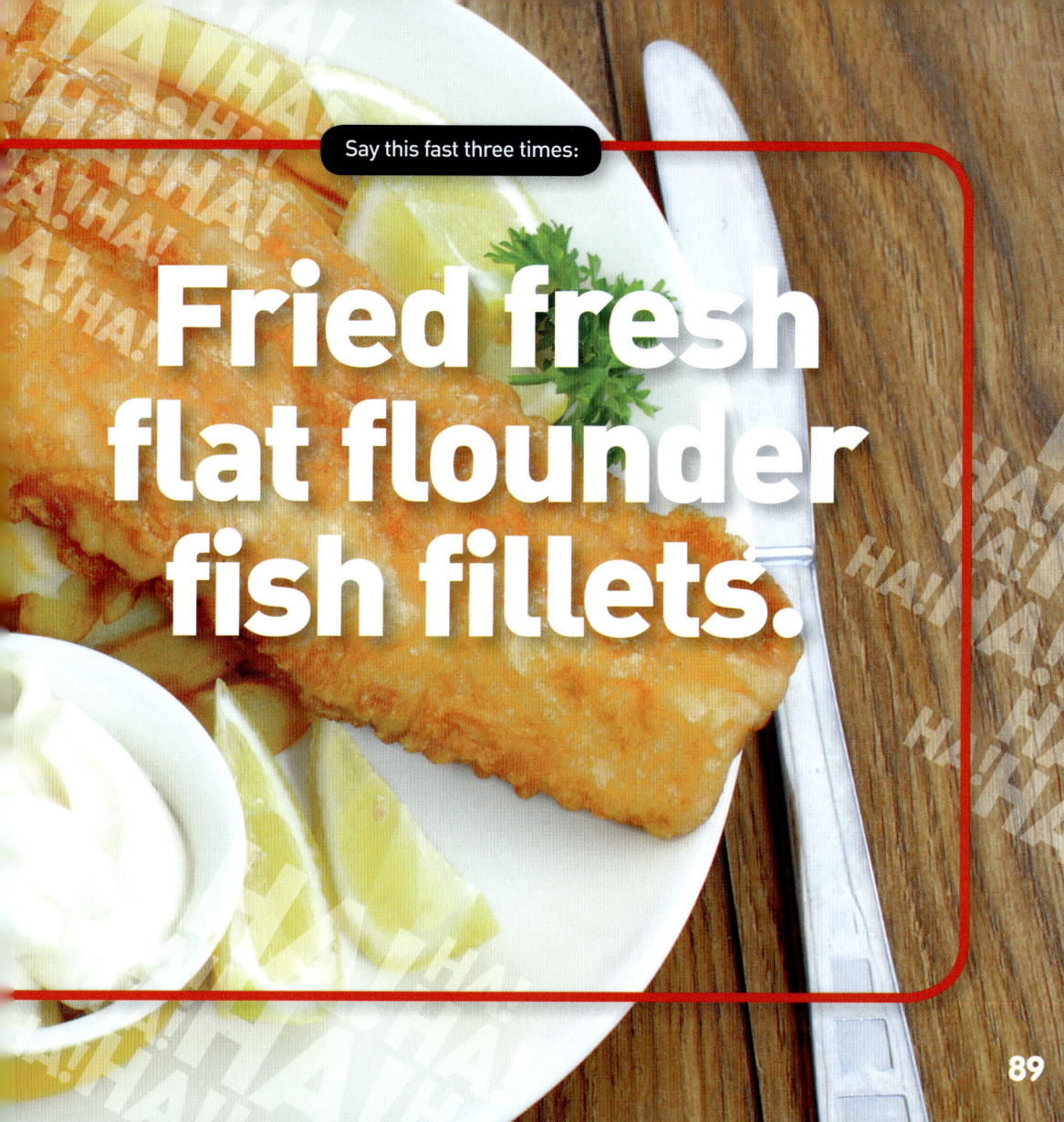

Say this fast three times:

Fried fresh flat flounder fish fillets.

What kind of trucks do dogs drive?

Range Rovers.

Q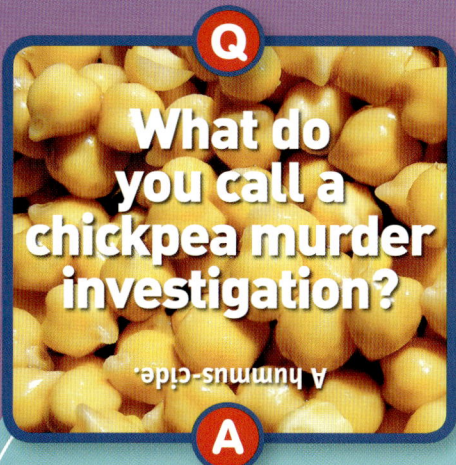

What do you call a chickpea murder investigation?

A A hummus-cide.

Q Why did the farmer give up training his pig to find buried mushrooms?

A Because it was more truffle than it was worth.

Q Why did the boxer put a banana in his glove?

So he could make fruit punch! **A**

TONGUE TWISTER!

Say this fast three times:

Faeries fight for food in Fernwood Forest.

FUNNY PUNS

A pig went to a party and drank four cups of punch. The host said, "Do you want to go to the bathroom before you leave?" The pig replied, "No thanks, I go wee wee wee all the way home."

Q

Why can't you make a **belt** out of **cardboard?**

Because it's a waist of paper.

A

Q

What do you get when you cross a cat and a tree?

A cat-a-log.

A

What do you
call a
hippo
that likes
**rap
music?**

A hip-hop-o-potamus.

HA! HA! HA! HA! HA! HA! HA! HA! HA! HA! HA! HA! HA! HA! HA! HA! HA!

KNOCK, KNOCK.

Who's there?
Adelia.
Adelia who?
Adelia in if you want to play cards.

Most fish do not have eyelids!

95

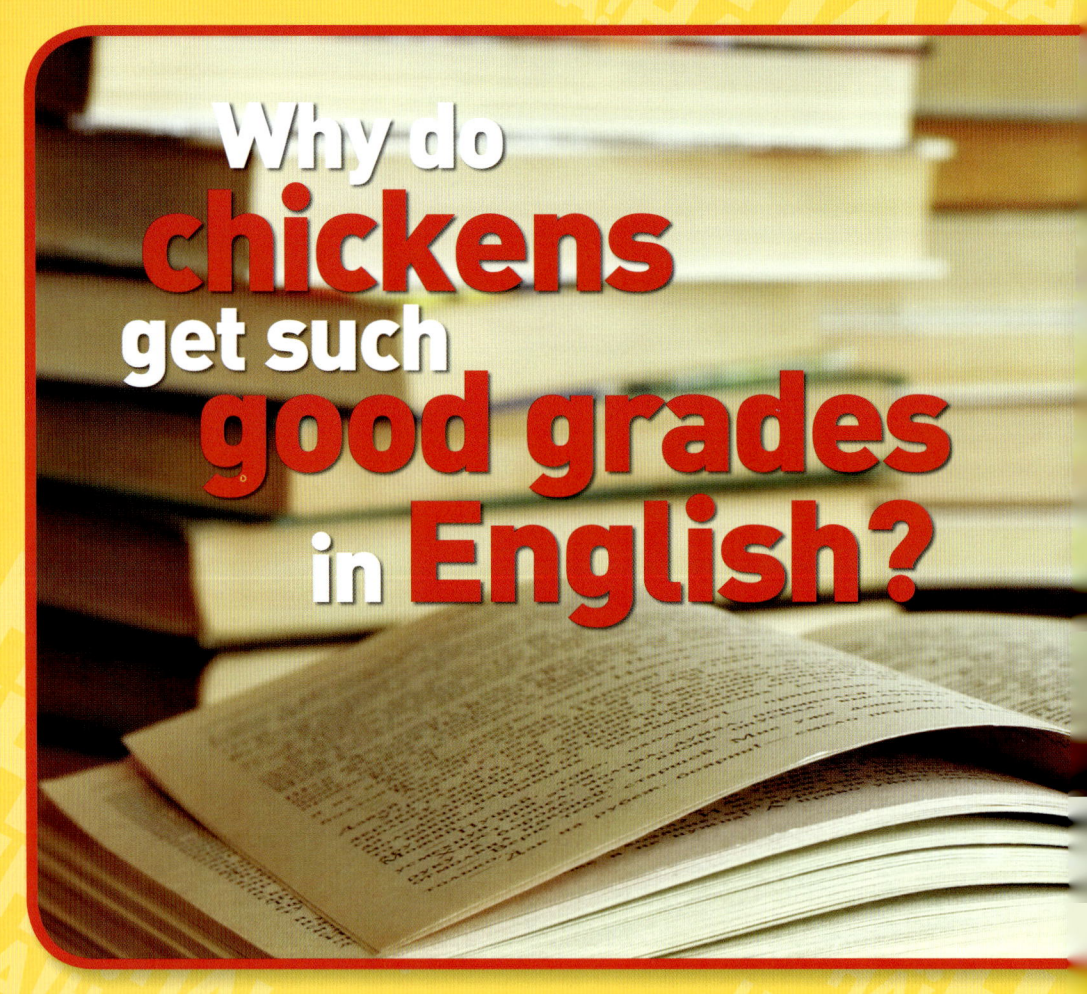

Why do **chickens** get such **good grades in English?**

Chickens are the most common bird, with over 25 billion in the world.

Because their grammar is im-peck-able.

Weddell seals can dive to depths up to 2,400 feet (750 m) and hold their breath for up to 80 minutes.

KNOCK, KNOCK.

Who's there?
Ron.
Ron who?
I tried to call but got the ron number!

Q What do you call a room full of jelly jars?

A Jam-packed.

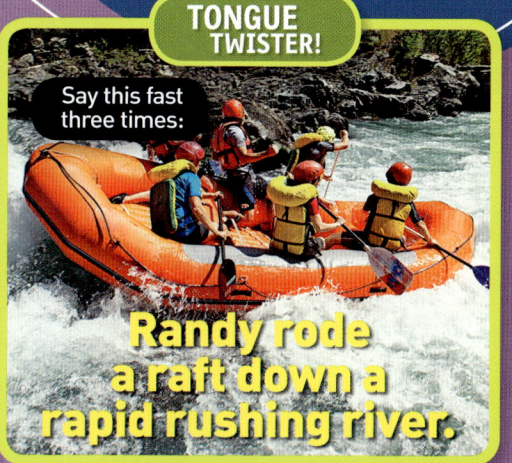

TONGUE TWISTER!

Say this fast three times:

Randy rode a raft down a rapid rushing river.

Q What do you call it when salt says hello to pepper?

A Season's greetings.

TONGUE TWISTER!

Say this fast three times:

Apes hate grape cakes.

Q Where can you find lots of bakeries?

A On the yeast coast.

Q Why did **Dracula** stand in the **road?**

A Because he heard there was a blood drive.

Baboons are also known as "dog-faced apes" because of their dog-like muzzles and large canine teeth.

KNOCK,

KNOCK.

Who's there?
Rome.
Rome who?
Rome is where the heart is.

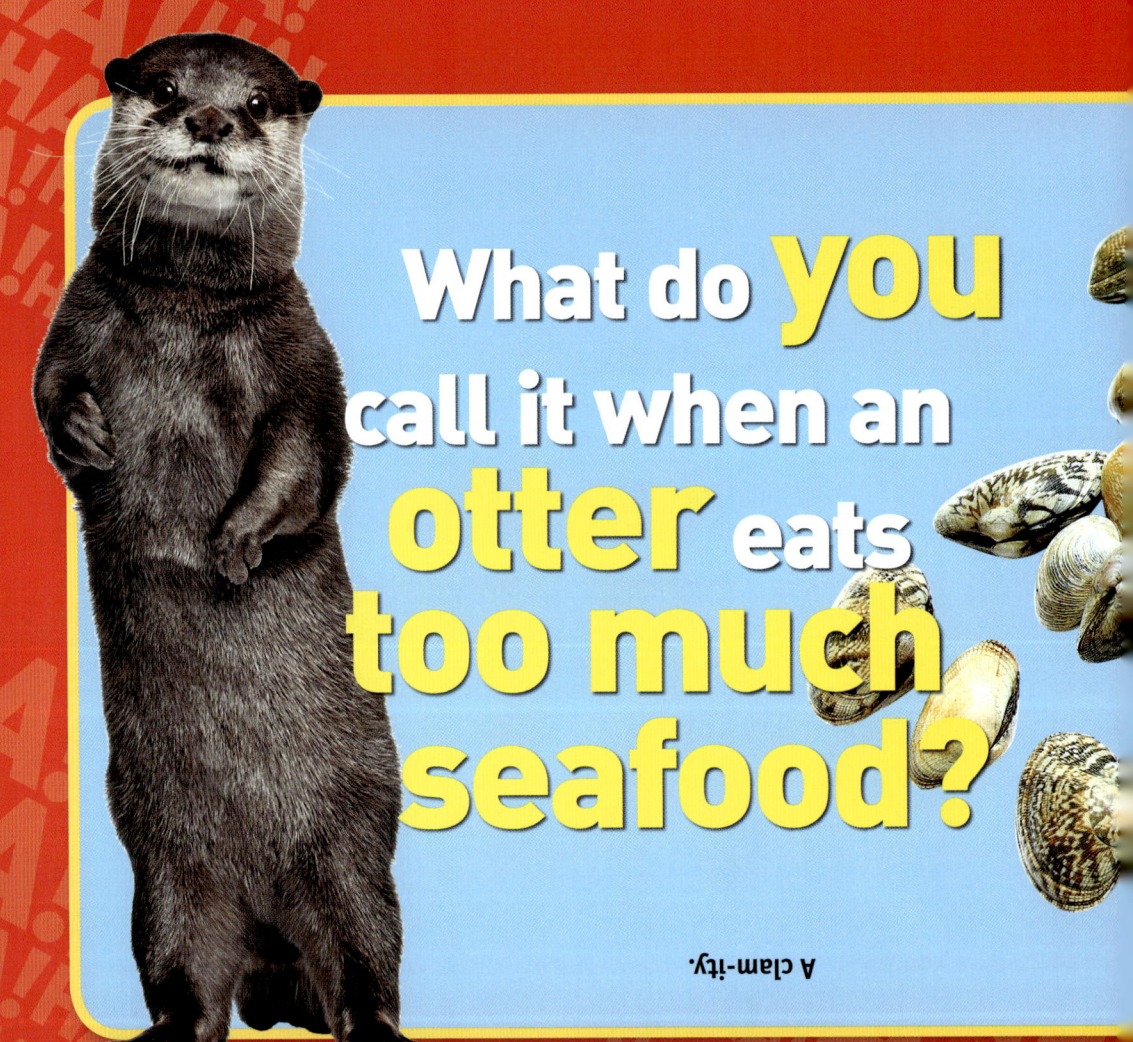

What do **you** call it when an **otter** eats **too much seafood?**

A clam-ity.

A female cat is called a queen and a male cat is called a tom.

104

Q What did the lamp say to the man?

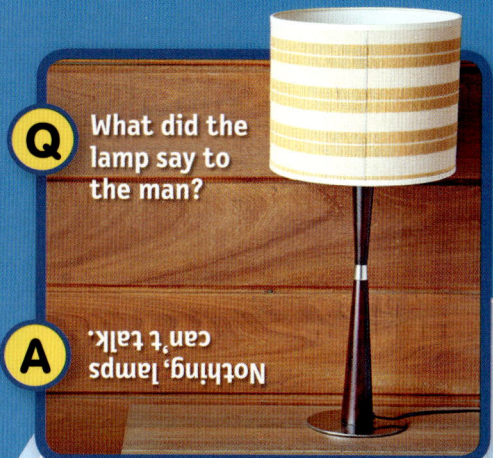

A Nothing, lamps can't talk.

Q What do you get if you cross a **shark** and a **parrot?**

A A bird that will talk your ear off.

TONGUE TWISTER!

Say this fast three times:

Seven swarthy swashbucklers sat swatting silly sand flies.

Q Why did the chicken cross the playground?

A To get to the other slide.

Q Why did the bee go to the doctor?

A Because she had hives.

Q What's a tornado's favorite game?

A Twister.

Q What do you call a **little green vegetable that runs away** from home?

A An esca-pea.

Q What do you call a mummy that does magic tricks?

A The Wizard of Gauze.

What do you do when a **pony** gets **sick?**

Send him to the horse-pital.

KNOCK, KNOCK.

Who's there?
Sara.
Sara who?
Sara 'nother way in?

Whales must be awake to breathe. This means they can never fall completely asleep or they will drown. Instead, they rest one half of their brain at a time!

What did the robber say when he held up the bakery?

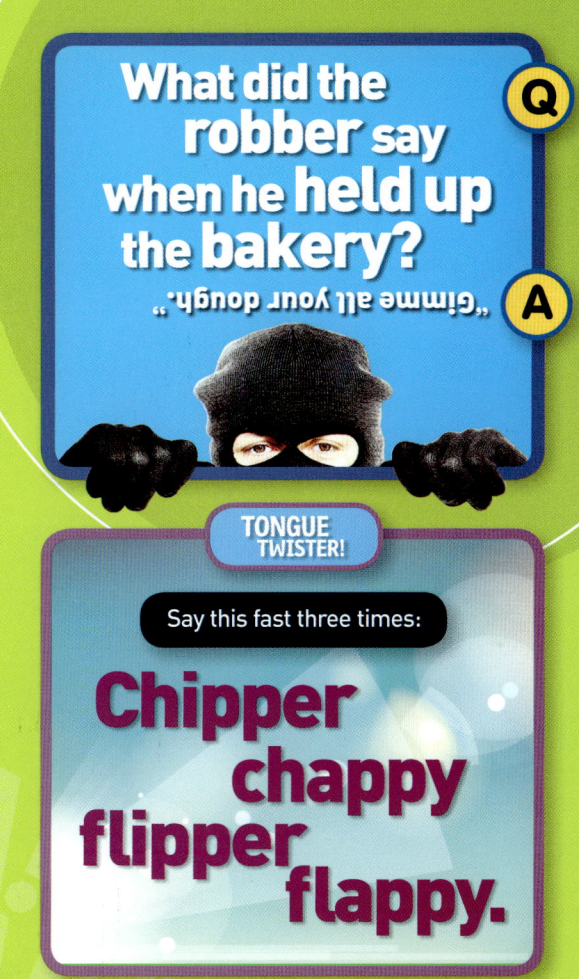

Q

A

"Gimme all your dough."

TONGUE TWISTER!

Say this fast three times:

Chipper chappy flipper flappy.

Young orangutans will live with their mothers for 11 to 12 years.

KNOCK, KNOCK.

Who's there?
Says.
Says who?
Says me, that's who!

Q What kind of TV shows do fish watch?

A Car-tunas.

Q How do you fix a broken tomato?

A With tomato paste.

Chihuahuas are descended from the Techichi, a dog beloved by people of the ancient Toltec civilization in Mexico.

KNOCK, KNOCK.

Who's there?
Pete.
Pete who?
Pete-za delivery guy!

What do you call a dinosaur with red hair?

Tri-carrot-tops.

Baby deer can take their first steps within a half hour of their birth.

KNOCK, KNOCK.

Who's there?
Sherry.
Sherry who?
Sherry your lunch?
I'm starving!

116

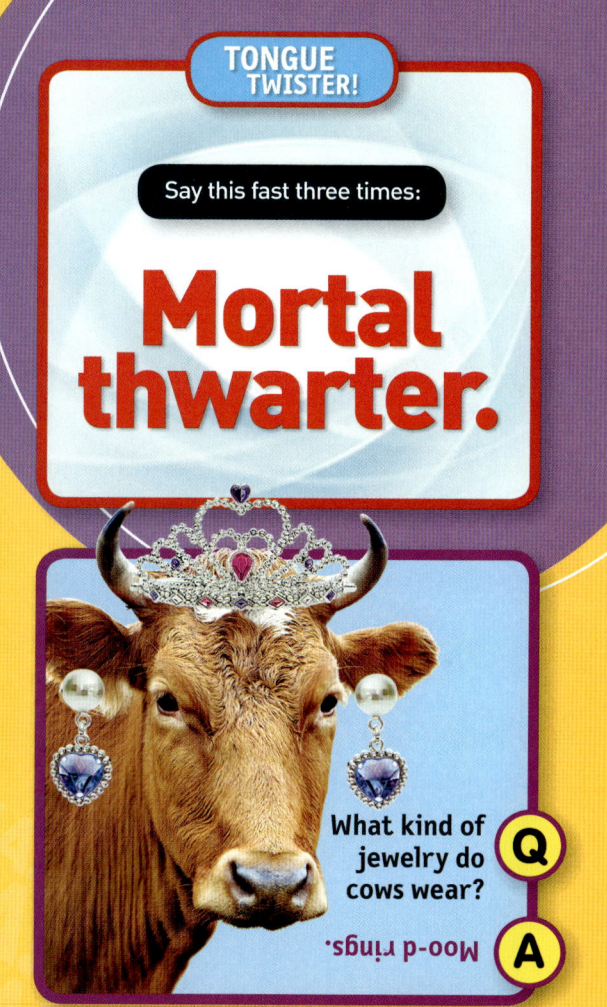

TONGUE TWISTER!

Say this fast three times:

Mortal thwarter.

Q What kind of jewelry do cows wear?

A Moo-d rings.

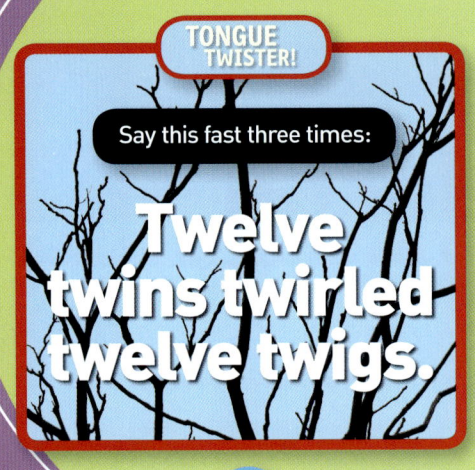

TONGUE TWISTER!

Say this fast three times:

Twelve twins twirled twelve twigs.

Q Who do apples call when there is an emergency?

A The pear-amedics.

Q Why are **people** always **so tired** in **April?**

A Because they just finished a March.

Q Why do tigers have stripes?

A So they don't get spotted

How does the
Easter Bunny
stay in shape?

He gets plenty of egg-cercise.

119

Pigs like to snuggle close together or even sleep nose to nose!

KNOCK, KNOCK.

Who's there?
Baby owl.
Baby owl who?
Baby owl see ya' later?

KNOCK, KNOCK.

Who's there?
Barbara.
Barbara who?
Barbara black sheep, have you any wool?

Don't surprise a momma grizzly bear! Grizzlies are known to be ferocious when protecting their young.

DYLAN:

Do you like selling coffee?

JOSH:

It has its perks.

Q Do cows like to dance?

A When they are in the moo-d.

Q

What kind of **shoes** does a **baker wear?**

A Loafers.

123

Q How do turtles talk to each other?

A On their shell phones.

Q What do you get if you cross a rabbit and a spider?

A A hare net.

TONGUE TWISTER!

Say this fast three times:

Pirate's private property.

Q What do you call two witches living in the same house?

A Broommates.

What kind of **dog** can **tell time?**

A watchdog.

How do you catch a squirrel?

Climb up a tree and act nuts.

Squirrels can fall up to 100 feet (30 m) without getting hurt! They use their tails as a parachute.

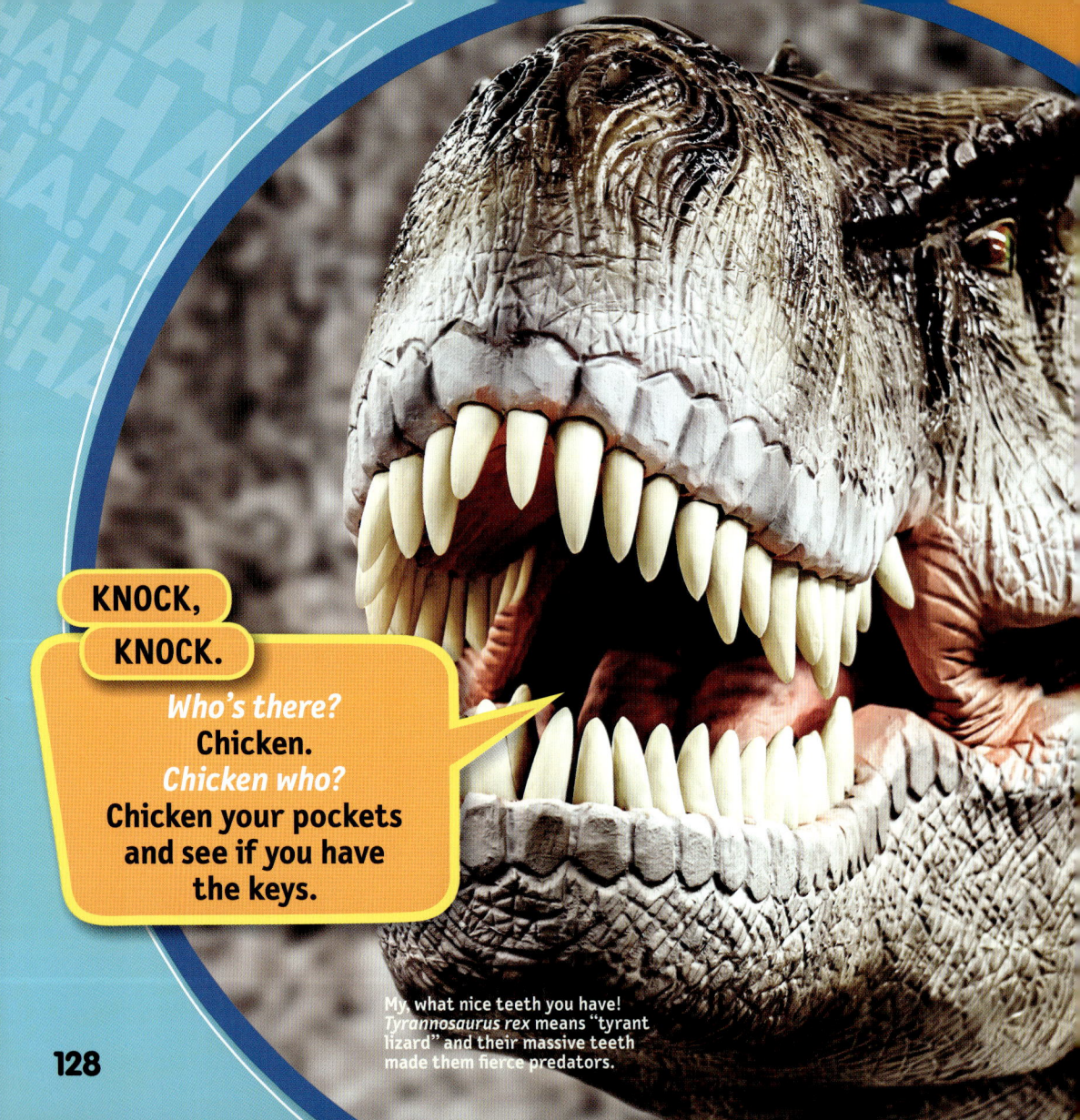

KNOCK, KNOCK.

Who's there?
Chicken.
Chicken who?
Chicken your pockets and see if you have the keys.

My, what nice teeth you have! *Tyrannosaurus rex* means "tyrant lizard" and their massive teeth made them fierce predators.

Q Where does a baby ghost sit at the dinner table?

A In a boo-ster seat.

TONGUE TWISTER!

Say this fast three times:

Upper roller, lower roller.

Q What kind of bird is always out of breath?

A A puffin.

CATHIE:
Did your party guests enjoy the piñata?

DOUG:
It was a huge hit!

Q What do you get if you cross a dog and a telephone?

A A golden receiver.

A bearded dragon can change its skin color to deflect the sun and prevent overheating.

KNOCK, KNOCK.

Who's there?
Answer.
Answer who?
Answer all over the picnic basket!

131

A panda's diet is made up almost entirely of bamboo. They will spend up to 12 hours a day eating it.

133

The red-eyed tree frog's brightly colored eyes and markings help to scare away predators.

Say this fast three times:

Two-toed tree toad.

Q What is a ghost's favorite cereal?

A Scream of wheat.

Q Why do birds fly south?

A Because it is too far to walk.

Q What **runs around** a **backyard?**

A A fence.

Q Where does Count Dracula eat his lunch?

A In the casketeria.

Say this fast three times:

Four furious fiends fought for freedom.

Q What kind of music does a mummy listen to?

A Wrap.

Pelicans use their long bills with expandable attached pouches to scoop up fish. They can eat many fish at a time.

KNOCK,

KNOCK.

Who's there?
Stan.
Stan who?
Stan back and I'll try the door again!

137

What is an **alien's** favorite chocolate?

A Milky Way bar.

Weighing in at a whopping 350 pounds (159 kg) and standing at 9 feet (2.9 m) tall, the ostrich is the largest bird of them all.

KNOCK, KNOCK.

Who's there?
Sven.
Sven who?
Sven are we leaving?

Q Why was the music teacher locked out of his classroom?

A The keys were on the piano.

Q What kind of dessert has a bad attitude?

A Apple grumble.

Q What do **snakes** do after they have a **fight?**

A Hiss and make up.

Q What **insect** is terrible at **football?**

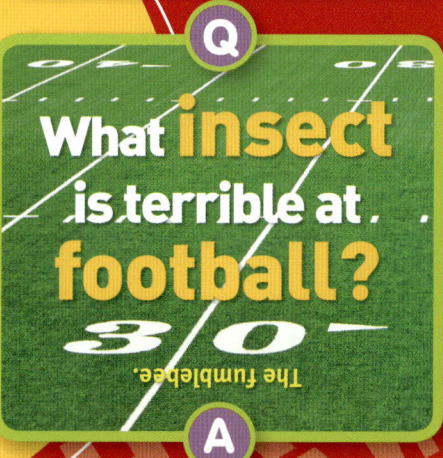

A The fumblebee.

Q What do nearsighted ghosts wear?

A Spook-tacles.

Q What is better than Christmas cookies?

A Christmas dough.

Q Why couldn't the monkey catch the banana?

A Because the banana split.

Q What can you hold without ever touching it?

A A conversation.

What do you get if you cross a gorilla and a pop singer?

Katy Hairy.

143

144

Polar bears are called
"nanooks" in the
Inuit language.

What do **hogs** do on a **Saturday** afternoon?

They go on a pignic.

KNOCK, KNOCK.

Who's there?
Twig.
Twig who?
Twig or tweet!

Meerkats are social animals. There can be up to 40 meerkats in one group.

Say this fast three times:

A noise annoys an oyster.

Q

What does a skeleton like to order at a restaurant?

A Spare ribs.

149

Q What is a dog's favorite holiday?

A Howl-o-ween.

Q How do you make a hot dog stand?

A Take its chair.

Q What do you get if you cross a chicken with a cement mixer?

A A brick-layer.

TONGUE TWISTER!

Say this fast three times:

A pack of pesky pixies.

What do you get when you cross a **cheetah** and a **french fry?**

Very fast food!

TONGUE TWISTER!

Say this fast three times:

Pop shop pop is tops.

Donkeys are strong! They can carry up to 30 percent of their body weight.

KNOCK, KNOCK.

Who's there?
Cargo.
Cargo who?
Cargo by, we better take the bus.

Q Why do people eat corn on the cob?

A Because it tastes a-maize-ing.

Q Did you hear the joke about the notebook?

A Never mind, it's tearable.

155

Q Why did the colander quit its job?

A It couldn't take the strain anymore.

Q Why are pirates called pirates?

A Because they arrrr!

Q What do you call two bakers trading buns?

A Roll reversal.

Q What do you call a shrimp that falls down a lot?

A Accident prawn.

Snowy owl babies are called owlets.

157

KNOCK, KNOCK.

Who's there?
Athena.
Athena who?
Athena shooting star!

Tokay geckos have a vicious bite. Luckily for humans, they eat insects.

Say this fast three times:

A cow crossed at a crowded cow crossing.

Q What kind of books do oranges read?

A Pulp fiction.

Q Why do **citrus fruits** like being the center of attention?

A Because they enjoy the limelight.

Q What do you call a deaf fish?

A Hard of herring.

Q Why doesn't it hurt to get hit with a can of soda?

A Because it's a soft drink.

Q Why didn't the man who ate a tube of glue tell anyone?

A Because his lips were sealed.

Q Why did the boy write his name on the neck of his shirt?

FRASER

A He wanted collar ID.

HA! HA! HA! HA! HA! HA! HA! HA! HA!

KNOCK, KNOCK.

Who's there?
Budda.
Budda who?
Budda this toast for me, please.

In addition to their distinctive egg-shaped heads, English bull terriers are the only recognized breed with triangular eyes.

TONGUE
TWISTER!

Say this fast three times:

Ten tiny terriers fought five feisty foxhounds.

Seeing spots? Leopard spots are called rosettes. Rosettes act as camouflage, helping leopards hide from larger prey in forests and grasslands.

KNOCK, KNOCK.

Who's there?
Fred.
Fred who?
Are you a-fred of ghosts?

Say this fast three times:

The ochre ogre over-ordered.

Why did the banana go to the hospital? **Q**

A Because it wasn't peeling well.

167

Koi fish are often kept in garden ponds. In the right conditions, they can live up to 25 years.

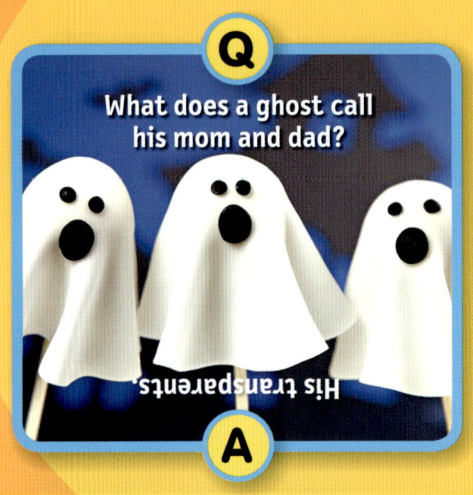

Q

What does a ghost call his mom and dad?

A

His transparents.

TONGUE TWISTER!

Say this fast three times:

Elsie ate elegant eggplant entrees.

Q What do you call a girl with broccoli in her ears?

A Anything you want, she can't hear you.

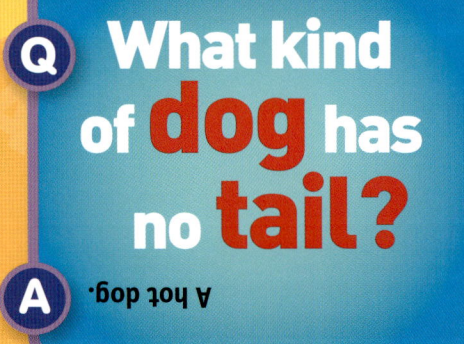

Q **What kind of dog has no tail?**

A A hot dog.

170

A **skunk** is an animal of great **dis-stink-tion.**

Skunks spray an oily liquid that can temporarily blind and stun other animals. It is strong enough to ward off bears!

171

Fuzzy Angora rabbit wool is removed by shearing or combing and used to make lightweight but warm sweaters.

Why was the rabbit so upset?

He was having a bad hare day.

Q What did the mother broom say to the baby broom?

A Time to go to sweep.

Q Why can't you move an envelope?

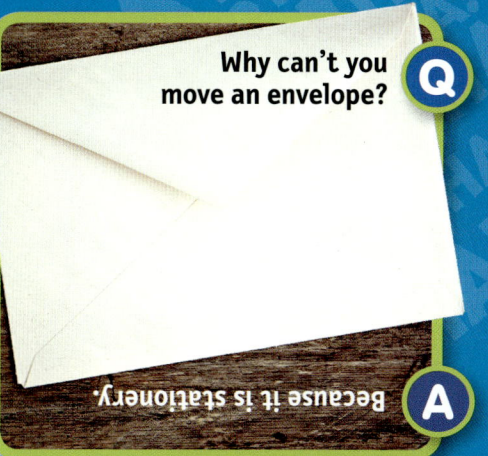

A Because it is stationery.

Q What do you call a thief who falls in wet cement?

A A hardened criminal.

TONGUE TWISTER!

Say this fast three times:

Russell wrangled wrestling rascals.

Q Why are horses such pessimists?

A Because they are neigh-sayers.

Q Why did the Velcro salesman quit his job?

A Because he couldn't stick with it.

Q What happened when the skunk fell in the swimming pool?

A It stank to the bottom.

Q What do you get if you put herbs in your computer's disk drive?

A A thyme machine.

KNOCK, KNOCK.

Who's there?
Eels.
Eels who?
My eels are killing me in these shoes.

Goats were the first animals humans used for milk.

Why did the **farmer** buy a **donkey?**

Donkeys have been used as working animals for over 5,000 years! A male donkey is a jack and a female is a jenny.

Because he thought he would get a kick out of it.

The hippopotamus is the third largest land mammal after the elephant and white rhinoceros.

KNOCK, KNOCK.

Who's there?
Fangs.
Fangs who?
Fangs sure aren't what they used to be.

Q Why is my dog so hot in the summertime?

A Because he wears a fur coat and pants.

Q What do you call it when a roller-skating bear falls down?

A A grizzly accident.

179

FUNNY PUNS!

LOUISE:
Do you like sushi?

TONY:
On rare occasions.

Q What do toads use in foggy weather?

A Their froghorns.

TONGUE TWISTER!

Say this fast three times:

Josh noshed posh squash.

A horse's hoof is like a fingernail. It must be clipped so the horse doesn't feel uncomfortable.

181

KNOCK, KNOCK.

Who's there?
Gnawing.
Gnawing who?
It's been nice gnawing you!

182

Seals are mammals that breed and look after their babies on land, but they spend the rest of their time in the ocean.

183

What is a vampire's favorite holiday?

Fangs-giving.

Q What do you call a cow with no legs?

A Ground beef.

JULIA: I fixed your torn denim pants.

EWAN: You are a jean-ius!

TONGUE TWISTER!

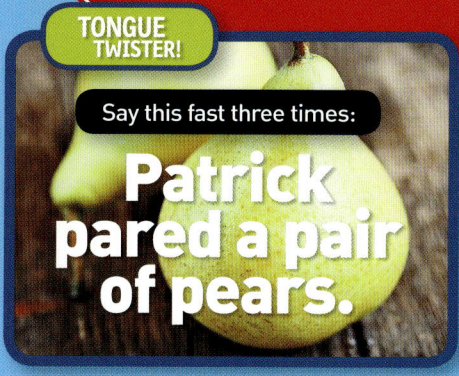

Say this fast three times:

Patrick pared a pair of pears.

Q Why was Cinderella thrown off the basketball team?

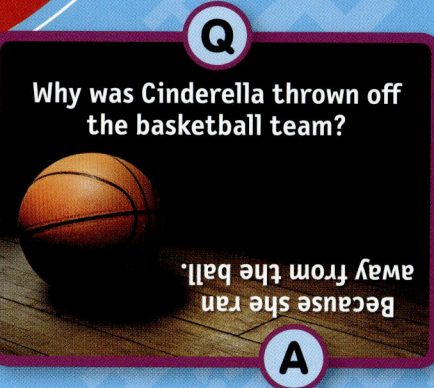

A Because she ran away from the ball.

Q

What kind of **room** has no **walls?**

A A mushroom.

Q Why do pilots worry about their jobs?

A Because their future is always up in the air.

Some chameleons can change their color to camouflage themselves when threatened, or as a reaction to temperature change.

KNOCK, KNOCK.

Who's there?
Stella.
Stella who?
Stella 'nother knock-knock joke.

187

TONGUE TWISTER!

Say this fast three times:

Beep bob bing bong bananas.

KNOCK,
KNOCK.

Who's there?
Wooden shoe.
Wooden shoe who?
Wooden shoe like
to go for a walk?

No two tigers have the
same stripe pattern.
They are as unique as a
human's fingerprints.

Q What was the eagle's reaction when he flew into a window?

A He felt hawkward.

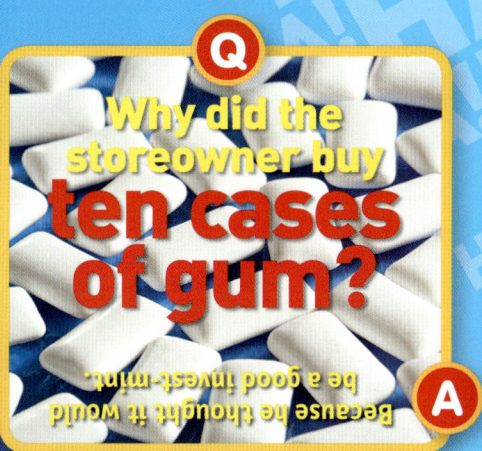

Q Why did the storeowner buy **ten cases of gum?**

A Because he thought it would be a good invest-mint.

Q Why should you **beware** of gangs of **coffee beans?**

A Because there's always trouble brewing.

LUMBERJACK 1: What was the best part of being a lumberjack?

LUMBERJACK 2: I saw the world.

Q

Why did the **barbers** join the **military?**

A They wanted to be in the hair force.

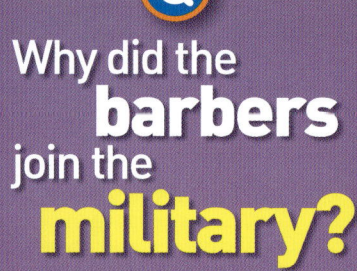

TONGUE TWISTER!

Say this fast three times:

The liniment is imminent.

Q Did you hear about the Oreo who got an A on his English test?

A He was one smart cookie!

Q Why did the news channel hire a leopard?

A Because they make great on-the-spot reporters.

KNOCK, KNOCK.

Who's there?
Myth.
Myth who?
I myth you too!

The caracal is an excellent acrobat. It can leap high into the air and catch a bird in flight!

Giraffes only sleep for about two hours a day. They usually curl up with their legs underneath them, but can also catch some z's standing up!

195

Huskies can have a range of eye colors: blue, brown, green, or gold. Some have one blue eye and one brown eye.

KNOCK, KNOCK.

Who's there?
Gorges.
Gorges who?
You look absolutely gorges!

196

JIM:
How was your flight?

NANCY:
It was just plane awesome!

TONGUE TWISTER!

Say this fast three times:

Furry felines fight fat ferrets.

TONGUE TWISTER!

Say this fast three times:

George ignored the boy cyborg.

Q

Did you hear the jester graduated from college?

A It was his clowning achievement.

Q

What did the dog tell his sweetheart on Valentine's Day?

A I Labradore you.

What do you call a **panda** that was tricked out of his **lunch?**

Bamboo-zled.

Their ability to imitate human speech has made parrots prized pets. Some also live for a long time — up to 80 years!

JOKEFINDER

JOKEFINDER

ILLUSTRATIONCREDITS

Published by the National Geographic Society

John M. Fahey, *Chairman of the Board and Chief Executive Officer*
Declan Moore, *Executive Vice President; President, Publishing and Travel*
Melina Gerosa Bellows, *Executive Vice President; Chief Creative Officer, Books, Kids, and Family*

Prepared by the Book Division

Hector Sierra, *Senior Vice President and General Manager*
Nancy Laties Feresten, *Senior Vice President, Kids Publishing and Media*
Jay Sumner, *Director of Photography, Children's Publishing*
Jennifer Emmett, *Vice President, Editorial Director, Children's Books*
Eva Absher-Schantz, *Design Director, Kids Publishing and Media*
R. Gary Colbert, *Production Director*
Jennifer A. Thornton, *Director of Managing Editorial*

Staff for This Book

Kate Olesin, *Project Editor*
David Seager, *Art Director*
Lisa Jewell, *Photo Editor*
Ariane Szu-Tu, *Editorial Assistant*
Callie Broaddus, *Design Production Assistant*
Margaret Leist, *Photo Assistant*
Grace Hill, *Associate Managing Editor*
Joan Gossett, *Production Editor*
Michael O'Connor, *Production Editor*
Lewis R. Bassford, *Production Manager*
Susan Borke, *Legal and Business Affairs*

Production Services

Phillip L. Schlosser, *Senior Vice President*
Chris Brown, *Vice President, NG Book Manufacturing*
George Bounelis, *Senior Production Manager*
Nicole Elliott, *Director of Production*
Rachel Faulise, *Manager*
Robert L. Barr, *Manager*

Editorial, Design, and Production by Plan B Book Packagers

The National Geographic Society is one of the world's largest nonprofit scientific and educational organizations. Founded in 1888 to "increase and diffuse geographic knowledge," the Society's mission is to inspire people to care about the planet. It reaches more than 400 million people worldwide each month through its official journal, *National Geographic*, and other magazines; National Geographic Channel; television documentaries; music; radio; films; books; DVDs; maps; exhibitions; live events; school publishing programs; interactive media; and merchandise. National Geographic has funded more than 10,000 scientific research, conservation and exploration projects and supports an education program promoting geographic literacy.

For more information, please visit nationalgeographic.com, call 1-800-NGS LINE (647-5463), or write to the following address:
National Geographic Society
1145 17th Street N.W.
Washington, D.C. 20036-4688 U.S.A.

Visit us online at nationalgeographic.com/books

For librarians and teachers: ngchildrensbooks.org

More for kids from National Geographic: kids.nationalgeographic.com

For information about special discounts for bulk purchases, please contact National Geographic Books Special Sales: ngspecsales@ngs.org

For rights or permissions inquiries, please contact National Geographic Books Subsidiary Rights: ngbookrights@ngs.org

Paperback ISBN: 978-1-4263-1504-6
Reinforced Library Binding ISBN: 978-1-4263-1505-3

Printed in China

15/PPS/1-BX